CHRIS DEVON

Real-Time Data Processing with Kafka

Contents

Introduction to Kafka and Real-Time Data Processing

I n today's digital landscape, the ability to process data in real-time has transformed industries, from finance and retail to logistics and social media. Real-time data processing refers to the capacity to ingest, process, and analyze data as it is generated, enabling organizations to respond instantly to events and trends. This capacity isn't just about speed; it's about gaining an advantage in decision-making, optimizing processes, and even predicting future behaviors based on live information.

Understanding Real-Time Data Processing

Historically, data processing has been segmented into two primary categories: batch and real-time processing. While batch processing—where data is processed in groups or "batches"—has long been the standard for many applications, it falls short in scenarios where data needs to be acted upon as soon as it arrives. Here, real-time processing is essential, enabling businesses to monitor events and gain insights in milliseconds rather than hours or days.

Real-time data processing, however, is technically challenging. For starters, it requires a framework capable of handling high-throughput data streams with low latency. Further, as the data grows in volume and variety, the system must stay resilient and ensure data consistency. This is where Apache Kafka emerges as a powerful solution, purpose-built for real-time data streaming.

Kafka Overview

Apache Kafka, developed initially at LinkedIn, was born out of the need to process vast amounts of event data in real time. Released to the open-source community in 2011, Kafka quickly gained traction for its ability to efficiently manage high-throughput, fault-tolerant, and distributed data streaming.

Kafka operates as a distributed messaging system, or more specifically, a distributed event streaming platform. Unlike traditional message brokers, which primarily handle point-to-point or publish-subscribe messaging patterns, Kafka excels at managing real-time data streams. It allows producers to publish data that consumers can subscribe to, making it possible to connect disparate systems, feed analytics, and enable reactive, data-driven applications.

Kafka's Role in Modern Data Infrastructure

As organizations increasingly embrace data-driven strategies, Kafka has become a foundational component of modern data infrastructures. Its unique design makes it suitable for a wide range of use cases, from log aggregation and user activity tracking to complex event processing in microservices.

Kafka's architecture is built to handle high throughput and scalability, making it ideal for companies that need to ingest millions of events per second. Moreover, Kafka integrates well with many big data tools and frameworks, providing seamless connectivity across data lakes, databases, and cloud platforms. This connectivity supports the integration of analytics pipelines and machine learning applications, further broadening Kafka's value in real-time data ecosystems.

Core Concepts of Kafka

To fully leverage Kafka, it's essential to understand its core concepts:

- **Topics:** Topics are the fundamental units in Kafka, representing channels through which data flows. A producer writes data to a topic, and a consumer reads from it. Each topic can be partitioned, allowing Kafka to scale horizontally by distributing data across multiple nodes.
- **Producers and Consumers:** Producers are clients that send data to

Kafka, while consumers are clients that read data. Kafka's design ensures that producers and consumers operate independently, meaning they don't directly communicate but instead interact with the Kafka server.

- **Partitions:** Kafka topics are divided into partitions, which enables parallelism. Each partition can be stored on different nodes, making it possible for Kafka to handle a large volume of data. Partitions are also the basis for data ordering within Kafka.
- **Brokers and Clusters:** Kafka is distributed across multiple servers called brokers. A collection of brokers forms a Kafka cluster. Each broker is responsible for handling the storage and retrieval of data, while the cluster manages data distribution, redundancy, and failover.

Understanding these core concepts will be essential as we delve deeper into Kafka's inner workings in later chapters, from handling complex data streams to integrating with other systems for enhanced functionality.

Kafka Ecosystem and Related Tools

Beyond Kafka itself, the Kafka ecosystem includes several tools that extend its functionality:

- **Kafka Connect:** Kafka Connect is a framework for integrating Kafka with external data systems, such as databases, file systems, and cloud storage. This framework enables Kafka to act as a bridge between systems, facilitating data ingestion and extraction without custom code.
- **Kafka Streams:** Kafka Streams is a lightweight, Java-based library for building stream-processing applications on top of Kafka. It provides capabilities for data transformation, aggregation, and filtering directly within Kafka, making it easier to build real-time analytics applications.
- **KSQL:** KSQL offers a SQL-like interface for querying and processing data stored in Kafka. By allowing users to express complex data flows with simple queries, KSQL makes it possible to build real-time applications without extensive programming.

Getting Started with Kafka

As we dive into Kafka's technical setup, it's essential to approach installation and configuration in a way that ensures smooth deployment, reliable performance, and scalability from the beginning. This chapter is structured to guide readers step-by-step through installing Kafka on various platforms, understanding basic CLI commands, and configuring Kafka for cloud deployment. With these skills, readers will be ready to initiate their Kafka environments, enabling a hands-on approach to real-time data streaming.

Installing and Setting Up Kafka Locally

Getting Kafka running on a local machine is the first step in familiarizing oneself with Kafka's architecture and operational flow. This section will walk readers through setting up Kafka on major operating systems.

- **Prerequisites and Environment Setup**
- Before installing Kafka, certain prerequisites must be in place. These include having Java Development Kit (JDK) installed, as Kafka is a Java-based application. Here, we'll cover:
- Installing JDK and verifying its version
- Installing ZooKeeper, which Kafka requires to manage broker coordination and leader elections. Kafka provides a built-in ZooKeeper, but users can also use an external one.
- **Step-by-Step Installation Guide for Windows, macOS, and Linux**
- **Windows Installation**

- We'll walk through downloading the Kafka binary, extracting the files, and setting up environment variables to facilitate easier command-line access.
- **macOS Installation**
- On macOS, installation can be simplified using tools like Homebrew. We'll cover the Homebrew installation process as well as manual setup for users who prefer it.
- **Linux Installation**
- We'll provide a step-by-step installation guide for Debian-based systems (Ubuntu) and Red Hat-based systems (CentOS), offering commands for a smooth installation process.
- **Starting Kafka and ZooKeeper Services** After installation, starting ZooKeeper and Kafka will be essential to confirm a successful setup. Here, we'll include instructions for launching these services and configuring them to run as background processes. This section will also explain the basic configuration files Kafka relies on and how to modify them for custom setups.

Understanding Kafka CLI and Basic Commands

Once Kafka is set up, understanding the Kafka Command Line Interface (CLI) enables users to interact directly with Kafka brokers, topics, producers, and consumers.

- **Managing Kafka Topics**
- Creating, listing, describing, and deleting topics.
- Explanation of topic configurations like partitions, replication factor, and retention policies. This section emphasizes how these configurations impact data throughput and availability.
- **Basic Commands for Producers and Consumers**
- Writing data to topics with producers and reading data with consumers.
- Examples will use simple data messages to illustrate the flow from producer to topic to consumer, helping users visualize Kafka's data streaming process.

- **Advanced CLI Usage and Scripts**
- Beyond basic commands, we'll cover useful CLI options like configuring offsets, setting up consumer groups, and managing offsets for replaying or skipping messages. Practical examples and use cases will showcase how these commands can be applied in a production setting.

Setting Up Kafka in the Cloud

For many applications, deploying Kafka in a cloud environment is ideal for scalability, flexibility, and resource optimization. This section will focus on deploying Kafka on popular cloud platforms, introducing readers to managed Kafka services as well as self-hosted options.

- **Deploying Kafka on AWS, Azure, and Google Cloud**
- Step-by-step guides for setting up Kafka on each cloud platform, including virtual machine configurations, storage considerations, and network settings to ensure optimal Kafka performance.
- Sample configurations for an enterprise-grade setup will be outlined, along with performance optimization tips specific to each cloud provider.
- **Managed Kafka Services: AWS MSK, Confluent Cloud, and Azure Event Hubs**
- **AWS Managed Streaming for Apache Kafka (MSK)**
- AWS MSK provides a managed Kafka environment that simplifies setup and maintenance. Here, we'll discuss configuration steps, scaling options, and monitoring tools unique to AWS MSK.
- **Confluent Cloud**
- As the company behind Kafka, Confluent offers a managed Kafka service that integrates seamlessly with their suite of tools. We'll explain how to set up a Confluent Cloud instance, manage billing, and integrate with other Confluent services like Kafka Streams and KSQL.
- **Azure Event Hubs for Kafka**
- Azure's Event Hubs service supports the Kafka API, allowing users to enjoy Kafka-like capabilities on a fully managed platform. This section will cover setup, resource scaling, and Event Hub's unique features,

including integration with Azure's analytics tools.

Common Configuration and Tuning for Performance

Getting Kafka running is one step, but fine-tuning configurations ensures stability, reliability, and performance. This section will provide tips for configuring Kafka's settings to handle varying workloads, especially in production environments.

- **Broker Configurations for Performance**
- We'll discuss settings like log.retention.ms, num.partitions, and replica.f etch.max.bytes, explaining how they impact performance and data durability.
- Tips for configuring storage and optimizing I/O performance, especially important in environments with high data throughput.
- **Consumer and Producer Tuning**
- Adjusting producer settings like acks, compression.type, and linger.ms to balance speed and reliability.
- Optimizing consumer configurations, including fetch.min.bytes, session.timeout.ms, and max.poll.records for efficient data processing.
- **ZooKeeper Considerations**
- Tuning ZooKeeper settings to handle Kafka's load, especially in large clusters.
- Monitoring ZooKeeper health and best practices for reducing ZooKeeper-related bottlenecks in Kafka deployments.

Kafka Fundamentals – Producers, Consumers, and Topics

Understanding Kafka's fundamentals—producers, consumers, and topics—is essential to grasping how data moves through Kafka's distributed system. This chapter breaks down each of these elements, providing practical examples and explanations of how they work individually and in unison to power real-time data streaming.

Producing Data to Kafka

Kafka's producers are responsible for sending data into the Kafka ecosystem. The efficiency and flexibility of Kafka's producers enable Kafka to handle a wide variety of data inputs with speed and resilience.

- **Introduction to Kafka Producers**
- Overview of the producer's role within Kafka's architecture.
- Benefits of asynchronous data production and how it impacts throughput and latency.
- **Configuring Producer Properties**
- Overview of essential producer configurations like acks, compression.type, retries, and linger.ms. Each of these settings can be adjusted to optimize data flow, reliability, and efficiency.
- Examples of different producer configurations for high-throughput vs. high-reliability scenarios.
- **Synchronous vs. Asynchronous Messaging**

- Explanation of Kafka's support for both synchronous and asynchronous data transmission.
- Trade-offs between the two modes and how each impacts performance, consistency, and message ordering.
- **Example: Writing Data to a Kafka Topic**
- Practical example illustrating how to set up a Kafka producer to write messages to a topic.
- Sample code snippets that demonstrate producing messages, with explanations for each line of code.

Consuming Data from Kafka

Consumers read data from Kafka topics, with Kafka offering significant flexibility in how data is consumed and managed. This section covers the nuances of setting up consumers, from individual consumers to consumer groups.

- **Understanding Consumer Basics**
- The role of consumers in Kafka and how they contribute to data processing.
- Introduction to consumer groups and how they allow for parallel data processing across multiple consumers.
- **Configuring Consumer Properties**
- Overview of key consumer configurations, including group.id, auto.off-set.reset, and enable.auto.commit.
- Examples of consumer configurations for scenarios requiring different levels of data consistency and fault tolerance.
- **Consumer Groups and Partition Assignment**
- Explanation of how consumer groups enable parallel processing within Kafka.
- How Kafka assigns partitions to consumers within a group, enabling scalability and redundancy.
- **Handling Offsets and Data Retention**
- Discussion on offset management and the importance of maintaining

offset consistency.
- Overview of Kafka's retention policies and how they impact data availability for consumers.
- **Example: Reading Data from a Kafka Topic**
- Sample code demonstrating how to set up a Kafka consumer and read data from a topic.
- Explanation of code snippets for reading data and handling offsets in real-time.

Kafka Topics and Partitions

Topics are Kafka's central abstraction, representing channels through which data flows from producers to consumers. Partitions within topics make Kafka scalable and ensure data is distributed efficiently across a cluster.

- **What Are Kafka Topics?**
- Introduction to topics as logical channels for data streaming.
- Explanation of how topics are structured and why they're essential for organizing data.
- **Partitioning for Scalability and Parallelism**
- Overview of how topics are divided into partitions, allowing for parallelism in data handling.
- Explanation of how partitions contribute to load balancing, fault tolerance, and scalability.
- **Data Ordering in Partitions**
- Discussion on Kafka's ordering guarantees within partitions.
- Scenarios where ordering is critical, and how Kafka's partitioning strategy maintains consistency.
- **Configuring Topic Properties**
- Overview of important topic configurations like num.partitions, replication.factor, and retention settings.
- Examples of topic configurations for different use cases, such as high-throughput streaming and fault-tolerant systems.

Data Serialization Formats

Kafka supports various serialization formats, which determine how data is encoded and decoded as it moves between producers, topics, and consumers. Choosing the right serialization format is crucial for ensuring compatibility and performance.

- **Introduction to Data Serialization**
- Explanation of serialization and its importance in Kafka.
- Overview of commonly used serialization formats: Avro, JSON, Protobuf, and XML.
- **Using Avro with Kafka**
- Introduction to Avro as a popular serialization format in Kafka.
- Explanation of Avro's schema evolution capabilities and compatibility features.
- **Schema Management with Kafka's Schema Registry**
- Introduction to Kafka's Schema Registry and its role in managing data schemas.
- Practical examples of registering schemas and enforcing schema compatibility across applications.

Practical Examples and Hands-On Exercises

To solidify understanding, this section provides hands-on exercises and practical examples. Readers will learn how to create producers and consumers, configure topics, and use different serialization formats in a working environment.

- **Building a Simple Producer-Consumer Application**
- Step-by-step guide for setting up a basic producer-consumer application.
- Instructions for producing and consuming messages with different configurations.
- **Exercises for Real-World Scenarios**
- Exercises simulating real-world use cases, such as handling data in a multi-consumer environment and managing offsets.

- Discussion of possible outcomes and troubleshooting tips for common issues.

Kafka's Distributed Architecture

K afka's distributed architecture underpins its ability to handle large
volumes of real-time data with reliability and fault tolerance. This
architecture comprises a network of brokers and clusters designed
to manage distributed data processing and storage efficiently. This chapter
explores how Kafka achieves its scalability and reliability goals through
partitioning, replication, leader election, and data durability strategies.

Kafka's Internal Mechanics: Brokers and Clusters
Kafka's brokers and clusters form the foundation of its distributed design.
Understanding how they work together is essential to grasping Kafka's
architecture.

- **Kafka Brokers: Roles and Responsibilities**
- Overview of Kafka brokers and their responsibilities, including handling
  client requests, managing data replication, and storing partition data.
- Explanation of broker configurations and settings that impact Kafka's
  performance, such as log.dirs for storage and num.io.threads for manag-
  ing client I/O.
- **Kafka Clusters and Data Distribution**
- Introduction to Kafka clusters as collections of brokers working together.
- How Kafka distributes data across multiple brokers to balance the load
  and achieve redundancy.
- Explanation of how Kafka scales horizontally, allowing additional
  brokers to be added to the cluster to support increased throughput.

- **Leader and Follower Roles in Partitions**
- Explanation of Kafka's leader-follower model, where each partition has one broker designated as the leader and the others as followers.
- Role of the leader broker in handling reads and writes, while followers replicate data to ensure fault tolerance.

Ensuring Fault Tolerance and High Availability

Kafka is designed to be fault-tolerant, ensuring data availability and consistency even if individual brokers fail.

- **Partition Replication for Redundancy**
- How Kafka uses replication to create multiple copies of each partition, improving data availability and durability.
- Overview of the replication.factor setting and its impact on data redundancy, fault tolerance, and resource usage.
- **In-Sync Replicas (ISR) and Data Consistency**
- Explanation of In-Sync Replicas (ISRs), which are brokers that have fully replicated the partition data and can serve as leaders if the current leader fails.
- How Kafka manages ISRs to maintain data consistency across replicas and ensure only up-to-date brokers handle data requests.
- **Leader Election and Failover**
- Discussion of Kafka's automated leader election process, which allows a follower to take over as leader if the current leader becomes unavailable.
- Overview of ZooKeeper's role in managing the leader election process and maintaining cluster metadata.

Data Durability and Retention Policies

Kafka's design ensures data durability, allowing it to store data reliably for extended periods. This section covers the mechanisms Kafka uses to ensure data persistence and manage data retention.

- **Kafka's Log-Based Storage System**

- Introduction to Kafka's log-based storage, where data is appended to logs on disk.
- Explanation of how log segments and indexes are used to efficiently store and retrieve data.
- **Configuring Retention Policies**
- Overview of Kafka's log.retention.ms, log.retention.bytes, and log.cleanup.policy settings, which control how long data is retained.
- Examples of different retention policy configurations, such as compacted logs for keeping the latest record version and deletion-based retention for time-sensitive data.
- **Log Compaction for Data Persistence**
- Explanation of log compaction as a mechanism for keeping the latest version of each unique key in a topic.
- Use cases where log compaction is beneficial, such as storing changelogs for databases or keeping a history of the latest customer transactions.

Managing Data Across Multiple Data Centers

For organizations with high availability requirements, deploying Kafka across multiple data centers provides additional fault tolerance and data redundancy.

- **Cross-Data Center Replication Strategies**
- Explanation of how Kafka can be set up for multi-data center replication, allowing data to be synchronized across geographically dispersed locations.
- Overview of mirror maker tools and alternative approaches for replicating data across Kafka clusters.
- **Ensuring Data Consistency Across Regions**
- Best practices for maintaining data consistency and latency in a multi-data center setup.
- How Kafka handles data synchronization across different regions, with an emphasis on trade-offs between consistency, availability, and latency.

Practical Examples and Hands-On Exercises

This section will give readers hands-on experience with configuring and managing Kafka's distributed architecture.

- **Setting Up a Kafka Cluster**
- Step-by-step instructions for configuring and launching a multi-broker Kafka cluster on a local machine or virtual environment.
- Practical exercises for setting up leader election, configuring ISRs, and testing failover scenarios.
- **Exercises in Partitioning and Replication**
- Example configurations to practice setting partition replication factors and managing data redundancy.
- Instructions for simulating broker failures and observing how Kafka handles leader election and replica synchronization.

Designing Real-Time Data Pipelines with Kafka

D esigning real-time data pipelines is fundamental to leveraging Kafka's power in data streaming. This chapter introduces readers to the principles and practices of pipeline design, covering Kafka's role as the backbone of data integration, transformation, and flow across systems. Through hands-on examples, readers will learn to set up reliable pipelines that integrate seamlessly with various data sources and sinks, while handling errors and ensuring data consistency.

Building a Basic Data Pipeline

Starting with the basics, readers will get familiar with the concept of a data pipeline and its components. This section will explain how Kafka acts as a conduit between data producers and consumers in a pipeline, ensuring data flows efficiently and reliably.

- **Introduction to Data Pipeline Design**
- Defining data pipelines and their role in real-time applications.
- Key components of a data pipeline: ingestion, processing, storage, and delivery.
- Kafka's role as a central hub for moving data between these components.
- **Designing a Simple Producer-Consumer Pipeline**
- Step-by-step guide to setting up a basic Kafka pipeline using a producer to ingest data and a consumer to process it.

- Configuring pipeline components to handle real-time data transfer from producer to consumer with minimal latency.
- **Best Practices for Reliable Pipeline Design**
- Strategies for designing pipelines that are resilient to failures and maintain data integrity.
- Common design patterns for Kafka-based data pipelines, such as single-stream, fan-out, and fan-in patterns.

Implementing Kafka Connect for Data Ingestion

Kafka Connect simplifies integrating external data sources into Kafka pipelines. This section will provide an overview of Kafka Connect and walk readers through using it to connect data sources like databases, file systems, and cloud services.

- **Overview of Kafka Connect**
- Introduction to Kafka Connect's architecture, with source and sink connectors.
- Benefits of using Kafka Connect for data ingestion, including scalability, flexibility, and minimal code requirements.
- **Setting Up Kafka Connect**
- Step-by-step instructions for installing and configuring Kafka Connect.
- Explanation of standalone vs. distributed modes, and when to use each.
- **Popular Connectors and Their Use Cases**
- Overview of commonly used connectors, such as JDBC for databases, HDFS for big data storage, and S3 for cloud storage.
- Use cases and examples for each connector type to illustrate real-world applications.
- **Configuring and Managing Connectors**
- Detailed guidance on configuring source and sink connectors for different data sources.
- Tips for managing connectors in production, including scaling, monitoring, and troubleshooting common issues.

Handling Errors and Fault Tolerance in Pipelines

Real-time data pipelines must be resilient to data errors and system failures. This section explores strategies for handling errors gracefully and building fault tolerance into Kafka pipelines.

- **Error Handling Strategies for Kafka Pipelines**
- Explanation of common error types in Kafka pipelines, including data format mismatches, timeouts, and connection issues.
- Techniques for capturing and logging errors without disrupting data flow.
- **Implementing Dead Letter Queues and Error Topics**
- Introduction to dead letter queues (DLQ) as a method for handling and rerouting problematic messages.
- Configuring Kafka topics specifically for error handling, allowing problematic messages to be revisited or corrected later.
- **Retry and Recovery Mechanisms**
- Strategies for implementing retry logic to automatically reprocess failed messages.
- Best practices for balancing retries with system performance and reliability.
- **Fault Tolerance with Kafka's In-Built Mechanisms**
- How Kafka's distributed architecture, with ISRs and partitioning, inherently supports fault tolerance.
- Configuring Kafka clusters for high availability and seamless failover in case of broker or partition failures.

Integrating Kafka with Data Processing Frameworks

To create end-to-end pipelines, Kafka often integrates with data processing frameworks such as Apache Spark, Flink, and Hadoop. This section will provide an introduction to these integrations and how they can be used to transform, aggregate, and analyze data within Kafka pipelines.

- **Overview of Apache Spark, Flink, and Hadoop Integration**

- Introduction to each framework's unique capabilities and how they complement Kafka in real-time data pipelines.
- Use cases where each framework excels, such as Spark for batch processing, Flink for stream processing, and Hadoop for large-scale data storage.
- **Using Kafka as a Data Source and Sink with Spark**
- Setting up Spark to read from and write to Kafka topics for real-time analytics.
- Sample code and configurations for integrating Kafka with Spark, including structured streaming.
- **Flink for Stateful Stream Processing with Kafka**
- Using Flink's capabilities for processing and aggregating data streams in real time.
- Examples of setting up Flink jobs that interact with Kafka to perform complex event processing and data transformations.
- **Hadoop Ecosystem Integration for Batch Processing and Storage**
- Using Kafka Connect to bridge Kafka with Hadoop, HDFS, or cloud storage solutions.
- Best practices for managing data flows between Kafka and batch processing/storage systems.

Practical Examples and Hands-On Exercises

This section will provide readers with practical exercises and examples to reinforce their understanding of real-time pipeline design with Kafka. Each exercise will focus on a specific aspect of pipeline configuration, error handling, or data integration.

- **Building a Producer-Consumer Pipeline with Kafka Connect**
- Step-by-step example of creating a simple producer-consumer pipeline with Kafka Connect for data ingestion.
- Configuring Kafka to handle data flow from a database source to a data warehouse sink.
- **Exercise: Configuring Dead Letter Queues**

- Practical exercise for setting up a dead letter queue and error handling topic.
- Testing the pipeline to simulate errors and observe how messages are rerouted for later handling.
- **Implementing a Multi-Framework Data Pipeline**
- Guide for setting up a multi-framework pipeline using Kafka, Spark, and Hadoop to handle real-time and batch processing in a single pipeline.
- Best practices for managing data flow, consistency, and performance across frameworks.

Real-Time Data Processing with Kafka Streams

K afka Streams offers a lightweight, Java-based library that integrates seamlessly with Kafka to provide real-time stream processing. Designed to be scalable, fault-tolerant, and easy to integrate, Kafka Streams transforms Kafka from a simple messaging system into a comprehensive platform for real-time data analytics and transformations. This chapter explores the fundamentals of Kafka Streams, its architecture, and the process of building data streaming applications using Kafka's Streams API.

Introduction to Kafka Streams

Kafka Streams is designed for developers who want to process and analyze data as it flows through Kafka. Unlike external stream processing systems like Spark or Flink, Kafka Streams is embedded within Kafka, making it ideal for microservices and real-time analytics where lightweight processing is required.

- **What is Kafka Streams?**
- Overview of Kafka Streams as a stream-processing library and how it fits into the Kafka ecosystem.
- Key advantages of Kafka Streams over other stream processing frameworks, including its lightweight, easy-to-deploy design and native integration with Kafka.

- **Use Cases for Kafka Streams**
- Examples of real-world applications that benefit from Kafka Streams, such as real-time data monitoring, anomaly detection, event-driven microservices, and fraud detection.
- Discussion on when to use Kafka Streams versus an external stream-processing tool like Apache Spark or Flink.

Kafka Streams Architecture and Processing Model

Understanding Kafka Streams' architecture is key to building efficient applications. This section covers the concepts of stream processing, the duality of tables and streams, and the unique architecture that enables Kafka Streams to process data in a distributed, fault-tolerant way.

- **Stream-Table Duality in Kafka Streams**
- Introduction to the stream-table duality concept, which is central to understanding how Kafka Streams processes and stores data.
- Explanation of how Kafka Streams uses streams and tables to handle both real-time events and persistent state.
- **Distributed Stream Processing in Kafka**
- Overview of how Kafka Streams distributes processing across multiple nodes and partitions for scalability.
- Explanation of parallelism and partitioning in Kafka Streams, allowing applications to scale based on data volume and processing needs.
- **Fault Tolerance and State Management in Kafka Streams**
- How Kafka Streams manages state with local state stores and Kafka changelog topics.
- Explanation of how state is replicated and recovered in case of application failure, ensuring data consistency and resilience.

Building Streaming Applications with Kafka Streams API

Kafka Streams provides an expressive API that simplifies the process of defining complex data flows and transformations. This section will cover the core components of the Kafka Streams API, including stream sources, transformations, and sinks.

- **Setting Up the Kafka Streams API**
- Steps for configuring and initializing a Kafka Streams application, including setting up properties like application ID, bootstrap servers, and state directory.
- Explanation of key API components: KStream, KTable, and GlobalK-Table.
- **Stream Transformations and Filtering**
- Overview of the map, flatMap, filter, and selectKey transformations, with examples of when and how to use each.
- Examples of using filtering and mapping to clean and enrich data in real time.
- **Windowing and Aggregations**
- Introduction to windowing and its importance in real-time applications that need to analyze data over a specific time frame.
- Explanation of tumbling, hopping, and session windows, with code examples demonstrating how to implement each type in Kafka Streams.
- Overview of aggregation operations like count, reduce, and aggregate for summarizing and analyzing data streams.
- **Joining Streams and Tables**
- Explanation of the different join types (inner join, left join, and outer join) and how they can be used to combine data from multiple streams or tables.
- Real-world use cases for stream-to-stream joins (e.g., combining logs from multiple sources) and stream-to-table joins (e.g., enriching events with static data).
- **Outputting Results to Kafka and External Systems**
- Configuring Kafka Streams to write processed data back to Kafka topics or to external systems using Kafka Connect.
- Example code for outputting results to different destinations, with considerations for maintaining data consistency.

Real-Time Analytics with Kafka Streams

Kafka Streams is well-suited for real-time analytics and monitoring applications, allowing businesses to derive insights from their data as it's produced.

- **Creating Real-Time Analytics Dashboards**
- Building a real-time analytics pipeline with Kafka Streams and visualizing the results with tools like Grafana or Kibana.
- Step-by-step example of processing raw data, performing aggregations, and delivering the results to a dashboard.
- **Monitoring and Anomaly Detection with Kafka Streams**
- Example use case of anomaly detection, where Kafka Streams processes data in real time to identify unusual patterns.
- Techniques for setting thresholds, creating alerts, and sending notifications based on real-time data.
- **Case Study: Real-Time Analytics in E-Commerce**
- A detailed case study showing how Kafka Streams can power real-time analytics in an e-commerce setting, such as monitoring customer activity, tracking inventory, and analyzing sales trends.

Practical Examples and Hands-On Exercises

This section will give readers hands-on experience with Kafka Streams, reinforcing the concepts and techniques covered in the chapter.

- **Building a Simple Data Transformation Application**
- Step-by-step guide for setting up a Kafka Streams application to read from a topic, apply transformations, and write the output to another topic.
- Sample code and explanation of each component, from stream definition to processing and output.
- **Exercise: Implementing a Real-Time Aggregation Pipeline**
- Exercise for creating a Kafka Streams application that aggregates data in real time, such as counting events by category or computing running

totals.

- Instructions for setting up windowing, aggregation, and output topics to observe the aggregation in real time.
- **Complex Use Case: Multi-Stream Join and Aggregation**
- Advanced exercise that combines multiple streams, performs joins, and outputs the results to a Kafka topic or external database.
- Real-world application scenario to practice advanced Kafka Streams concepts and API usage.

Kafka's Role in Event-Driven Architectures and Microservices

E vent-driven architecture (EDA) has become essential for building flexible, decoupled applications, allowing systems to react to events as they happen. Kafka's robust messaging capabilities, fault tolerance, and high throughput make it an ideal platform for supporting EDA in microservices. In this chapter, readers will learn how Kafka functions within event-driven systems, enabling microservices to communicate asynchronously and respond to events in real time.

Kafka as the Backbone of Event-Driven Systems

In an event-driven architecture, events trigger actions and data flows across multiple components. Kafka enables this by acting as an event broker, allowing microservices to publish and subscribe to events independently of one another.

- **Introduction to Event-Driven Architectures**
- Overview of EDA, its benefits in modern software architecture, and key principles like loose coupling, responsiveness, and scalability.
- Types of events in EDA: state change events, transactional events, and entity events.
- How Kafka's distributed, pub-sub model is ideal for event-driven systems, providing a scalable backbone for event propagation and processing.
- **Benefits of Using Kafka in EDA**

- Key advantages of using Kafka in EDA, such as durability, scalability, and high throughput.
- How Kafka helps decouple services by providing asynchronous communication, making it easier to add, remove, or modify services without disrupting the whole system.
- Examples of how Kafka's fault-tolerant design and data retention policies contribute to reliable, event-driven applications.

Designing Microservices with Kafka

Kafka plays a central role in enabling event-driven microservices, allowing services to communicate asynchronously while remaining loosely coupled. This section introduces best practices for designing microservices with Kafka as the messaging backbone.

- **Introduction to Microservices Architecture**
- Overview of microservices architecture, its advantages over monolithic systems, and the key principles: single responsibility, independence, and resilience.
- How microservices communicate and coordinate with Kafka, facilitating event-based interactions rather than direct calls.
- **Event-Driven vs. Request-Response Architectures**
- Differences between event-driven (asynchronous) and request-response (synchronous) architectures, including their strengths and weaknesses.
- Scenarios where event-driven microservices excel, such as high-load environments, decoupled components, and complex workflows.
- **Implementing Event Sourcing with Kafka**
- Introduction to event sourcing and how Kafka can act as a durable event log, storing a history of all changes to system state.
- Explanation of how event sourcing works with Kafka topics, allowing services to rebuild state by replaying events.
- Practical example: using Kafka to maintain an event-sourced application where data changes are captured as a series of events.
- **Using Kafka for Command Query Responsibility Segregation**

(CQRS)

- Explanation of CQRS and its role in separating command and query responsibilities in microservices.
- How Kafka can facilitate CQRS by serving as the event store for commands and a notification mechanism for changes in state.
- Use case example of a CQRS-based microservices architecture with Kafka, demonstrating command handling and real-time updates.

Designing and Implementing Event Notifications and Event Processing

Event notifications and event processing are essential patterns in EDA, allowing systems to react to real-time changes without direct communication between services. Kafka supports these patterns with its robust messaging and distributed processing capabilities.

- **Implementing Event Notifications with Kafka**
- Overview of how Kafka topics can serve as notification channels between microservices, ensuring that events are reliably delivered.
- Best practices for designing notification topics, including topic naming conventions, partitioning strategies, and consumer group configurations.
- **Handling Event Processing and Data Enrichment**
- Techniques for processing and enriching data in an event-driven system with Kafka.
- How Kafka Streams can be used to transform, filter, and aggregate events as they flow through the system.
- Real-world example of an event processing pipeline where incoming events are enriched with metadata before being passed to other services.
- **Maintaining Data Consistency in Distributed Systems**
- Challenges of ensuring data consistency in a distributed, event-driven environment.
- Techniques for maintaining eventual consistency in microservices with Kafka, including idempotency, deduplication, and handling duplicate events.
- Explanation of how Kafka's consumer groups and offset management

can help manage consistency across distributed services.

Building Resilient and Scalable Event-Driven Systems with Kafka

Resilience and scalability are critical for any distributed system, especially in a microservices environment. Kafka's architecture provides built-in mechanisms to support these qualities, ensuring that event-driven applications are robust and capable of handling large data volumes.

- **Strategies for Scaling Kafka in Microservices**
- Configuring Kafka to handle increased data load and growing service demands, including horizontal scaling with more partitions and brokers.
- Optimizing Kafka's performance in high-load microservices environments, including best practices for partitioning and resource allocation.
- **Fault Tolerance and Recovery in Event-Driven Architectures**
- Techniques for designing fault-tolerant services that can recover from failures without losing data or functionality.
- How Kafka's replication, failover, and offset management features contribute to system resilience.
- Example scenarios where Kafka helps maintain system stability, such as handling network outages, hardware failures, and service crashes.
- **Building Idempotent Event Handlers and Processing Logic**
- Ensuring that event processing is idempotent to avoid issues from duplicate events.
- Techniques for making Kafka consumers idempotent, ensuring that operations like database writes, updates, and state changes are only applied once per event.

Case Studies and Real-World Applications

To provide practical insights, this section will explore real-world examples of how companies use Kafka to implement event-driven microservices and meet specific business requirements.

- **Case Study 1: Real-Time Order Processing in E-Commerce**

- Overview of how an e-commerce platform uses Kafka to process orders in real time, from placing an order to inventory and shipment updates.
- Explanation of how Kafka enables asynchronous communication between order, inventory, payment, and shipping services.
- **Case Study 2: Monitoring and Alerting in Financial Services**
- How a financial institution leverages Kafka to process real-time transaction data, monitor for anomalies, and trigger alerts.
- Description of the event-driven design that enables rapid detection and response to suspicious activity without affecting transaction performance.
- **Case Study 3: Event-Driven Customer Analytics in Retail**
- How Kafka supports real-time customer behavior tracking, enabling a retail company to perform data analytics and generate insights into customer interactions.
- Explanation of how Kafka handles the high volume of customer events, supports analytics in real time, and powers personalization algorithms.

Practical Examples and Hands-On Exercises

This final section provides hands-on exercises to solidify readers' understanding of Kafka in event-driven microservices.

- **Building a Simple Event-Driven Microservices System with Kafka**
- Step-by-step guide for setting up a basic event-driven system with two or three microservices communicating through Kafka topics.
- Instructions for configuring Kafka topics, creating events, and handling inter-service communication.
- **Exercise: Implementing Event Sourcing with Kafka**
- Example of implementing a simple event-sourcing pattern with Kafka, capturing state changes as a series of events.
- Practical steps to replay events and rebuild service state in a microservices environment.
- **Implementing a Notification System with Kafka**
- Exercise to set up a notification system where microservices communi-

cate through Kafka topics for event-based notifications.

- Example of handling different types of notifications, such as order updates, account alerts, and customer support messages.

Advanced Kafka Features for Real-Time Data Processing

A
s real-time data processing requirements grow, advanced Kafka configurations and features become essential for building efficient, secure, and resilient applications. This chapter explores Kafka's capabilities for enhancing security, managing data schemas, implementing exactly-once processing, and optimizing performance, enabling developers to handle sophisticated use cases with confidence.

Kafka Security Essentials

Security is a critical aspect of any distributed system, especially when sensitive data is transmitted. Kafka provides several security features to protect data and ensure secure communication.

- **Securing Data with SSL and SASL**
- Overview of SSL (Secure Sockets Layer) and SASL (Simple Authentication and Security Layer) as methods for encrypting data in transit and securing client-broker communications.
- Step-by-step guide to setting up SSL for Kafka, including generating SSL certificates, configuring brokers, and enabling SSL for client connections.
- Explanation of SASL mechanisms (PLAIN, GSSAPI, OAUTHBEARER) for authentication and how to set up SASL to authenticate users connecting to Kafka.
- **Implementing Role-Based Access Control (RBAC) with ACLs**

- Overview of Access Control Lists (ACLs) in Kafka and how they provide fine-grained permissions for users and services.
- Examples of creating ACLs for different roles (producer, consumer, administrator) and how to restrict access based on topics, groups, and operations.
- Best practices for managing ACLs in large organizations, including strategies for minimizing administrative overhead.
- **Configuring Authentication and Authorization for Multi-Tenant Environments**
- How to implement secure multi-tenant setups in Kafka, allowing multiple teams or organizations to use Kafka without compromising data security.
- Explanation of how to isolate tenant data, configure authentication for each tenant, and manage permissions using ACLs.

Managing Data Schema Evolution

Kafka's ability to handle schema evolution is crucial in real-time data applications where data structures change over time. The Schema Registry and other schema management tools ensure data consistency and compatibility across evolving data formats.

- **Using Confluent Schema Registry**
- Introduction to the Schema Registry and its role in managing data schemas for Kafka topics.
- Explanation of how Schema Registry works with Avro, JSON, and Protobuf schemas to enforce schema compatibility.
- Setting up the Schema Registry and configuring Kafka producers and consumers to register and validate schemas automatically.
- **Schema Compatibility Modes**
- Overview of the different compatibility modes available in Schema Registry: backward, forward, and full compatibility.
- Explanation of when to use each compatibility mode and the trade-offs involved.
- Practical examples of schema evolution scenarios, such as adding,

removing, or modifying fields, and how compatibility modes affect application stability.

- **Best Practices for Schema Evolution**
- Strategies for evolving schemas in a controlled manner, including versioning and documentation.
- Tips for managing schema changes in distributed teams to minimize data inconsistencies.
- Common pitfalls in schema evolution and how to avoid breaking changes when updating schemas.

Configuring Exactly-Once Processing in Kafka

Exactly-once processing ensures that messages are delivered and processed exactly once, a critical requirement for systems where data duplication can lead to inaccuracies and inconsistencies. Kafka's exactly-once semantics provide a way to achieve this in real-time data pipelines.

- **Understanding Kafka's Exactly-Once Semantics**
- Introduction to exactly-once processing, including the concept of idempotency and its role in maintaining data accuracy.
- How Kafka's exactly-once semantics differ from at-least-once and at-most-once processing.
- **Implementing Transactional Messaging with Kafka**
- Explanation of Kafka's transactional API and how it enables exactly-once processing for producers and consumers.
- Step-by-step guide to creating transactional producers, beginning and committing transactions, and ensuring that messages are processed once per consumer group.
- Examples of implementing exactly-once semantics in applications that handle financial transactions, inventory management, or other critical operations.
- **Best Practices for Exactly-Once Processing in Real-Time Applications**
- Techniques for ensuring idempotency in message processing, such as

using unique identifiers or deduplication keys.

- Configurations and tuning tips to reduce latency and maintain high throughput while using exactly-once semantics.
- Example use cases where exactly-once processing adds significant value, such as banking and real-time analytics.

Optimizing Performance and Resource Allocation

Kafka's performance can be fine-tuned for high-throughput, low-latency applications, making it suitable for demanding real-time data processing environments. This section explores best practices for configuring Kafka to maximize performance.

- **Configuring Broker Settings for Optimal Performance**
- Key Kafka broker configurations that impact performance, including num.network.threads, num.io.threads, log.segment.bytes, and log.retention.ms.
- Tips for balancing memory, CPU, and storage to achieve efficient data handling and prevent bottlenecks.
- Practical examples of tuning broker settings for different workloads, such as high-throughput data ingestion vs. low-latency message delivery.
- **Optimizing Producer and Consumer Configurations**
- Overview of producer configurations like acks, linger.ms, and batch.size, and how they impact throughput and latency.
- Configuring consumers for optimal performance, including settings like fetch.min.bytes, max.poll.records, and session.timeout.ms.
- Real-world examples of producer and consumer configurations that maximize resource efficiency and data flow.
- **Using Kafka's Built-In Metrics for Monitoring and Profiling**
- Explanation of Kafka's built-in metrics system, including key performance metrics for brokers, topics, and clients.
- How to use monitoring tools (e.g., Prometheus, Grafana) to track Kafka's performance, identify bottlenecks, and prevent performance degradation.

- Examples of profiling Kafka's performance in production environments and actionable insights based on common metric patterns.

Practical Examples and Hands-On Exercises

This final section will provide hands-on examples and exercises for implementing advanced Kafka features, giving readers practical experience with Kafka's security, schema management, exactly-once processing, and performance tuning.

- **Exercise: Setting Up SSL and ACLs for Secure Kafka Communication**
- Step-by-step guide for setting up SSL for secure communication between Kafka brokers and clients.
- Configuring ACLs to enforce role-based access control, testing different roles and permissions.
- **Implementing Exactly-Once Processing in a Sample Application**
- Practical exercise for creating a Kafka application that uses exactly-once semantics.
- Example scenario where exactly-once processing is necessary, and instructions for testing idempotency and transaction consistency.
- **Optimizing Kafka for High-Throughput Data Ingestion**
- Hands-on example for configuring Kafka brokers, producers, and consumers to handle high-throughput workloads.
- Testing and benchmarking Kafka performance with different configurations, analyzing the impact of each setting.

Deploying and Managing Kafka in Production

D eploying Kafka in production requires careful planning, robust configuration, and ongoing management to ensure consistent performance and reliability. This chapter walks through the process of setting up a Kafka cluster for production use, monitoring its health and performance, scaling the deployment as data demands grow, and maintaining stability through proactive management.

Best Practices for Kafka Production Deployments

Deploying Kafka in production environments necessitates best practices that emphasize resilience, efficiency, and maintainability.

- **Setting Up Kafka for High Availability**
- Configuring Kafka clusters with a sufficient number of brokers to ensure high availability.
- Overview of replication factor settings and partition management to handle failover scenarios effectively.
- Tips for setting up multi-node ZooKeeper clusters to support Kafka's high availability.
- **Partitioning and Replication Strategies**
- Designing partitioning strategies that optimize Kafka's scalability and load distribution.
- Choosing the right replication factor for each topic based on data

importance and required availability.
- Balancing partition distribution across brokers to prevent performance bottlenecks and ensure fault tolerance.
- **Hardware and Resource Configuration**
- Recommendations for Kafka broker hardware, including CPU, memory, storage, and network resources.
- Storage best practices, such as using SSDs for fast access times and RAID configurations for data redundancy.
- Configuring server resources for predictable Kafka performance, including buffer sizes, thread counts, and disk I/O optimization.

Monitoring and Performance Tuning

Continuous monitoring and performance tuning are essential for maintaining Kafka's stability and performance in production. This section covers Kafka's monitoring tools, metrics, and techniques for diagnosing and resolving performance issues.

- **Using Prometheus and Grafana for Kafka Monitoring**
- Setting up Prometheus to collect Kafka metrics, including broker, topic, and consumer metrics.
- Configuring Grafana dashboards to visualize Kafka performance and identify potential bottlenecks.
- Key Kafka metrics to monitor in production, such as message throughput, consumer lag, disk utilization, and memory usage.
- **Understanding and Managing Consumer Lag**
- Explanation of consumer lag and its impact on Kafka's real-time data processing capabilities.
- Techniques for managing and reducing consumer lag, including tuning consumer configurations and balancing partition assignments.
- Troubleshooting consumer lag issues in high-load environments and best practices for minimizing lag.
- **Profiling and Diagnosing Bottlenecks**
- Using Kafka's built-in metrics and tools to identify performance bottle-

necks in brokers, topics, and clients.

- Step-by-step guide to profiling Kafka performance and analyzing resource utilization patterns.
- Example scenarios of common performance bottlenecks, such as network saturation and disk I/O issues, with solutions for each.

Scaling Kafka Clusters for High Availability

Scaling Kafka clusters is essential as data volumes grow, ensuring the system can handle increased load while maintaining high availability and reliability.

- **Horizontal Scaling Strategies for Kafka**
- Best practices for adding brokers to a Kafka cluster to handle additional data and user demands.
- Steps for partition reassignment and balancing load across new brokers.
- Tips for ensuring a smooth scaling process, including rolling upgrades and minimizing downtime.
- **Configuring Multi-Region Kafka Deployments**
- Overview of setting up Kafka across multiple data centers or cloud regions for high availability.
- Techniques for replicating data between regions using Kafka Mirror-Maker or Confluent's multi-region architecture.
- Handling data consistency and latency issues in multi-region deployments.
- **Considerations for Autoscaling in Cloud Environments**
- Introduction to autoscaling Kafka in cloud environments, using AWS, Azure, or Google Cloud.
- Best practices for configuring auto-scaling triggers based on Kafka metrics, such as throughput and lag.
- Tips for managing costs and resource allocation in autoscaling Kafka deployments.

Backup, Restore, and Disaster Recovery Planning

Production environments require robust backup and disaster recovery strategies to protect data and ensure business continuity.

- **Setting Up Kafka Backups**
- Different approaches for backing up Kafka data, including using file-based storage, cloud backups, and third-party tools.
- Tips for automating Kafka backups and ensuring backups are consistent and reliable.
- Recommendations for backup frequency and retention policies based on data sensitivity and regulatory requirements.
- **Restoring Kafka Data After Failures**
- Step-by-step guide for restoring Kafka data from backups after broker failures or data corruption.
- Techniques for recovering topics, partitions, and offsets to ensure consistency across producers and consumers.
- Example scenarios for partial and full restores and considerations for minimizing data loss.
- **Implementing Disaster Recovery Plans for Kafka**
- Key components of a disaster recovery (DR) plan, including failover strategies, data replication, and recovery time objectives (RTO).
- Explanation of Kafka's disaster recovery features, including cross-data-center replication and high-availability configurations.
- Testing and validating DR plans to ensure they are effective in a real-world event, such as a major outage or data center failure.

Managing Kafka Cluster Updates and Maintenance

Regular maintenance and updates are essential to keep Kafka clusters secure, performant, and compatible with evolving infrastructure and application needs.

- **Planning and Executing Rolling Upgrades**
- Step-by-step guide to performing rolling upgrades on a Kafka cluster with minimal downtime.
- Best practices for upgrading Kafka versions, including compatibility

checks, testing, and monitoring during the upgrade process.

- Explanation of ZooKeeper compatibility and upgrade steps for both Kafka and ZooKeeper.
- **Kafka Configuration Management in Production**
- Managing configuration changes in production environments, including strategies for testing and deploying changes safely.
- Using tools like Kafka Config Provider and centralized configuration management solutions to simplify configuration updates.
- Common configuration settings to optimize in production, such as log retention, replication, and topic quotas.
- **Regular Maintenance and Monitoring Tasks**
- Checklist of routine Kafka maintenance tasks, such as checking disk space, monitoring resource usage, and balancing partitions.
- Strategies for ensuring cluster health, including log compaction, cleaning up old topics, and pruning unnecessary data.
- Practical tips for avoiding common maintenance pitfalls, like underestimating storage needs or neglecting monitoring.

Practical Examples and Hands-On Exercises

To reinforce the concepts covered in this chapter, this section includes practical exercises and examples for deploying, monitoring, and managing Kafka in production.

- **Exercise: Setting Up a Multi-Broker Kafka Cluster**
- Step-by-step guide to configuring and deploying a multi-broker Kafka cluster in a production-like environment.
- Instructions for configuring brokers, setting up replication, and verifying cluster health.
- **Monitoring Kafka with Prometheus and Grafana**
- Practical exercise for setting up Prometheus and Grafana to monitor Kafka metrics.
- Configuring alerts for key metrics, such as consumer lag and disk usage, to notify the team of potential issues.

- **Implementing a Disaster Recovery Plan**
- Example scenario for setting up a disaster recovery plan, including backup and restore configurations.
- Testing the DR plan by simulating a broker failure and verifying data consistency and recovery.

Real-World Use Cases of Kafka Across Industries

K afka's flexibility and robustness have made it a go-to solution for real-time data streaming across industries. In this chapter, readers will explore how Kafka is deployed to address specific business challenges, with case studies in e-commerce, finance, IoT, healthcare, and more. These use cases highlight Kafka's role in enabling event-driven architectures, real-time analytics, and scalable data pipelines.

Kafka in E-Commerce: Real-Time Customer Analytics

E-commerce platforms rely on real-time data to understand customer behavior, manage inventory, and optimize user experience. Kafka's ability to handle high volumes of streaming data makes it ideal for e-commerce applications.

- **Tracking Customer Behavior in Real Time**
- How Kafka is used to stream clickstream data, track user sessions, and gather insights into user behavior.
- Example of using Kafka to process data for personalized recommendations, abandoned cart recovery, and product recommendations.
- Explanation of a customer analytics pipeline that ingests data from web and mobile sources, processes it in real time, and feeds it to analytics systems.
- **Managing Inventory and Supply Chain in Real Time**

- Overview of real-time inventory management powered by Kafka, allowing e-commerce platforms to monitor stock levels, predict shortages, and reorder supplies dynamically.
- Example of using Kafka to connect inventory systems, supply chain partners, and warehouse management, ensuring up-to-date information across all channels.
- **Case Study: Building a Real-Time Recommendation System**
- Detailed case study of an e-commerce platform using Kafka to deliver personalized recommendations based on real-time user activity.
- Step-by-step process of setting up the recommendation engine, from data ingestion to processing and delivering recommendations.

Kafka in Finance: Fraud Detection and Risk Analysis

The finance industry demands real-time processing to detect fraudulent activities, manage risk, and meet regulatory requirements. Kafka's low-latency and fault-tolerant design enable financial institutions to process large volumes of transactions and detect anomalies as they happen.

- **Real-Time Fraud Detection Using Kafka**
- How Kafka is employed to stream transaction data in real time, monitoring for patterns indicative of fraudulent behavior.
- Techniques for integrating Kafka with machine learning models that analyze data on the fly to identify suspicious transactions.
- Example of using Kafka's exactly-once semantics to ensure consistent transaction processing for fraud detection applications.
- **Risk Analysis and Portfolio Management**
- Overview of Kafka's role in aggregating and analyzing data from multiple sources to assess portfolio risk in real time.
- Explanation of how Kafka helps investment firms manage real-time data streams, including stock prices, news, and economic indicators, to inform trading decisions.
- **Case Study: Kafka-Driven Risk Monitoring and Alerts System**
- Case study of a financial institution that uses Kafka to power a risk

monitoring system, aggregating data from multiple sources and alerting analysts to market shifts.

- Implementation details on how the system processes data, triggers alerts, and ensures data integrity across real-time and historical analysis.

Kafka in IoT: Processing Sensor Data at Scale

The Internet of Things (IoT) relies heavily on real-time data ingestion and processing, as devices continuously generate data that needs to be processed, analyzed, and stored. Kafka's scalability and ability to manage high-throughput data streams make it ideal for IoT applications.

- **Ingesting and Analyzing IoT Sensor Data with Kafka**
- How Kafka is used to collect and process data from a vast array of IoT sensors, from industrial equipment to smart home devices.
- Explanation of Kafka's role in managing data pipelines that transform raw sensor data into actionable insights.
- Use case example of a smart city application where Kafka aggregates data from sensors across the city for real-time monitoring and analytics.
- **Building a Scalable IoT Data Pipeline**
- Overview of a scalable IoT data pipeline architecture using Kafka, allowing companies to handle data from millions of connected devices.
- Techniques for managing and partitioning IoT data in Kafka to ensure low-latency data processing and long-term storage.
- Example of integrating Kafka with time-series databases and machine learning models to predict equipment failures.
- **Case Study: Kafka-Driven Predictive Maintenance in Manufacturing**
- Real-world example of a manufacturing company using Kafka to monitor equipment health and predict failures before they occur.
- Explanation of the predictive maintenance pipeline, from sensor data ingestion to real-time processing and alerting.

Kafka in Healthcare: Real-Time Data Processing and Patient Monitoring

Healthcare organizations use Kafka to manage and analyze patient data, ensuring timely insights for patient care and operational efficiency. Kafka enables real-time data processing, helping healthcare providers make informed decisions faster.

- **Kafka for Real-Time Patient Monitoring**
  - How Kafka facilitates real-time data collection and analysis for monitoring patient vitals, such as heart rate, blood pressure, and oxygen levels.
  - Explanation of how Kafka integrates with healthcare systems to alert medical staff to critical changes in patient status.
  - Example of a patient monitoring pipeline where Kafka ingests data from medical devices and delivers it to healthcare providers for analysis.
- **Integrating Kafka with Electronic Health Records (EHR)**
  - Overview of Kafka's role in synchronizing patient data across hospitals, clinics, and labs, ensuring seamless EHR integration.
  - How Kafka ensures secure, compliant data transfers in healthcare environments, meeting standards such as HIPAA.
- **Case Study: Kafka for Real-Time Health Analytics and Alerts**
  - Case study of a healthcare provider using Kafka to support real-time analytics, such as patient monitoring, clinical data aggregation, and alerts.
  - Implementation details on how Kafka powers data flows across different systems, ensuring accurate, up-to-date health data.

Kafka in Telecommunications: Network Monitoring and Customer Insights

In the telecommunications industry, Kafka helps manage large volumes of data generated by network devices, user activity, and customer interactions, providing real-time insights for network monitoring and customer experience optimization.

- **Network Monitoring and Fault Detection**
  - How Kafka is used to collect and process data from network infrastructure in real time, enabling rapid fault detection and resolution.
  - Explanation of Kafka's role in aggregating data from network devices,

analyzing performance metrics, and identifying potential network issues.
- **Customer Analytics and Personalization**
- Overview of how telecommunications companies use Kafka to analyze customer interactions and personalize service offerings.
- Example of a Kafka-based system that collects data on user activity, processes it in real time, and applies insights to improve customer retention and satisfaction.
- **Case Study: Kafka for Real-Time Network Monitoring and Service Optimization**
- Detailed case study of a telecommunications company using Kafka to monitor network performance and optimize service delivery.
- Description of the system's architecture, from data ingestion to real-time alerting and reporting.

Practical Exercises and Hands-On Examples

To reinforce these use cases, this section provides hands-on examples and exercises that demonstrate Kafka's real-world applications across industries.

- **Exercise: Building a Real-Time Analytics Pipeline for E-Commerce**
- Step-by-step guide for setting up an analytics pipeline that tracks customer activity and provides real-time insights.
- Instructions for ingesting data from a mock e-commerce website, processing it with Kafka Streams, and visualizing analytics in a dashboard.
- **Exercise: Implementing a Fraud Detection Pipeline in Finance**
- Exercise for creating a fraud detection pipeline that ingests transaction data, processes it in real time, and identifies potential fraud.
- Example code and configuration for setting up Kafka with machine learning models for anomaly detection.
- **Exercise: IoT Data Processing Pipeline for Predictive Maintenance**
- Practical example of setting up an IoT data pipeline that collects sensor data from industrial equipment and processes it for predictive maintenance.
- Instructions for configuring Kafka topics, ingesting data, and integrating

with a time-series database for long-term analysis.

Best Practices and Advanced Techniques for Kafka

Running Kafka in production environments requires more than just a basic understanding of configuration. As systems scale and data volume increases, adhering to best practices and implementing advanced techniques ensures Kafka operates efficiently, remains resilient, and can handle complex workloads. This chapter explores advanced configuration, data consistency, fault tolerance, and scaling strategies to help readers maximize Kafka's capabilities.

Optimizing Data Retention and Compaction

Kafka's data retention policies and compaction settings significantly impact performance, storage, and application behavior. Understanding and configuring these options is crucial for balancing resource usage with data accessibility.

- **Configuring Data Retention for Efficiency**
- Overview of Kafka's data retention settings, including log.retention.ms, log.retention.bytes, and log.cleanup.policy.
- How to balance retention times with storage costs based on application requirements, such as keeping short-term data for analytics while archiving long-term data.
- Examples of retention settings for different use cases, including transactional data, user activity logs, and historical records.

- **Using Log Compaction for Data Persistence**
- Explanation of Kafka's log compaction feature, which keeps the latest record of each unique key, making it ideal for applications that only require the most recent data.
- Configuring log compaction policies to handle use cases like changelogs for databases or tracking the latest state of user profiles.
- Best practices for setting up compaction, including how to manage compaction frequency and avoid performance bottlenecks.
- **Retention Policies for Data Archiving and Compliance**
- Strategies for implementing data retention that align with compliance requirements, such as GDPR or HIPAA.
- Practical examples of data archiving setups, including exporting older data to cloud storage or using Kafka Connect to offload data from Kafka topics.

Data Consistency and Ordering in Kafka

Maintaining data consistency and ordering is critical in distributed systems, especially for applications that rely on precise event sequences. This section covers techniques for ensuring consistent data processing and managing ordering guarantees within Kafka.

- **Achieving Exactly-Once Processing in Kafka**
- Review of exactly-once semantics in Kafka, including how they ensure data accuracy in systems where duplicate events could cause issues.
- Explanation of Kafka's transactional API and idempotent producers, enabling applications to write data with exactly-once guarantees.
- Practical example of using exactly-once processing in financial transactions to avoid discrepancies and maintain auditability.
- **Ordering Guarantees and Partitioning Strategies**
- Explanation of Kafka's partitioning model and its impact on data ordering within topics.
- Strategies for designing partitioning to maintain ordering across specific keys or within particular event streams.

- Techniques for ensuring ordering consistency in multi-consumer scenarios, including using consumer groups and partition affinity.
- **Handling Idempotency in Consumer Applications**
- Importance of idempotency in consumer applications to prevent duplicate processing, especially in fault-tolerant or retry scenarios.
- Techniques for designing idempotent consumers using unique identifiers or database constraints.
- Example scenarios where idempotency is necessary, such as data ingestion for analytics and processing logs for auditing.

Building Fault-Tolerant Kafka Applications

Kafka is inherently fault-tolerant, but implementing fault tolerance effectively requires configuring applications and brokers to handle failures gracefully. This section explores fault-tolerant design patterns and configurations that ensure data availability and resilience.

- **Leveraging Kafka's Replication for Fault Tolerance**
- Overview of Kafka's replication model, including how leader and follower replicas provide redundancy.
- Configuring replication factors and ISR (In-Sync Replicas) settings to maximize fault tolerance without sacrificing performance.
- Explanation of Kafka's failover mechanisms, ensuring that replicas can take over seamlessly if a broker goes down.
- **Designing Resilient Consumers and Producers**
- Best practices for designing producers and consumers that can handle failures without data loss, including using acknowledgments (acks), retries, and error handling.
- Techniques for configuring consumer applications to recover from failures, such as checkpointing and handling offsets.
- Practical example of a fault-tolerant consumer that can resume processing after network outages or server crashes.
- **Implementing Dead Letter Queues for Error Handling**
- Using dead letter queues (DLQ) to handle problematic messages that

cannot be processed, ensuring they do not disrupt the main data pipeline.
- Strategies for configuring Kafka topics as DLQs, where failed messages can be analyzed or retried later.
- Example of a DLQ setup for a microservices environment, where failed events are routed to a dedicated topic for further processing.

Concurrency and Scaling Patterns in Kafka

Kafka's design allows for parallel data processing, but managing concurrency and scaling effectively requires specific patterns and configurations. This section will guide readers in maximizing Kafka's parallel processing capabilities.

- **Parallel Processing with Partitioning and Consumer Groups**
- Explanation of Kafka's partitioning model and how consumer groups allow for parallel processing of data across multiple instances.
- Best practices for configuring consumer groups to balance load across consumers, avoiding overloading individual consumers.
- Example of scaling consumer applications with partitioning, showing how to distribute processing load dynamically as data volume grows.
- **Optimizing Throughput and Latency for High-Volume Applications**
- Techniques for optimizing producer and consumer configurations to increase throughput, such as adjusting linger.ms, batch.size, and fetch.min.bytes.
- Best practices for reducing latency, including using appropriate compression settings, managing buffer sizes, and balancing network resources.
- Practical example of tuning Kafka for a high-volume data pipeline that requires both high throughput and low latency.
- **Handling Concurrency in Event-Driven Architectures**
- Patterns for handling concurrency in event-driven microservices using Kafka, including event sourcing and CQRS (Command Query Responsibility Segregation).
- Tips for managing concurrency when multiple consumers process events

asynchronously, ensuring data consistency and avoiding race conditions.
- Example use case of a concurrent microservices system with Kafka, demonstrating partitioning and consumer group configurations.

Practical Examples and Hands-On Exercises

This final section provides hands-on exercises and practical examples to help readers apply advanced Kafka techniques in real-world scenarios.

- **Exercise: Configuring Data Retention and Compaction**
- Step-by-step guide to setting up retention and compaction policies for Kafka topics.
- Instructions for testing different retention settings and observing compaction behavior on sample data.
- **Exercise: Implementing Exactly-Once Processing in a Real-World Scenario**
- Practical exercise for setting up exactly-once processing with Kafka's transactional API.
- Example scenario where exactly-once semantics are necessary, such as financial transactions, with instructions for testing consistency and error handling.
- **Exercise: Building a Fault-Tolerant Data Pipeline with Dead Letter Queues**
- Instructions for setting up a data pipeline with dead letter queues for error handling and fault tolerance.
- Steps to test the pipeline under different failure scenarios and verify data recovery using DLQs.
- **Exercise: Tuning Kafka for High-Volume Concurrency**
- Configuring Kafka brokers, producers, and consumers to handle high-concurrency workloads.
- Testing Kafka's throughput and latency with concurrent consumers, observing the impact of different configurations on performance.

Emerging Trends and Future Directions in Kafka

T he landscape of data streaming is rapidly evolving, and Kafka remains at the forefront. With advancements in cloud-native technology, event-driven architectures, real-time analytics, and machine learning, Kafka continues to adapt to meet the demands of modern applications. In this chapter, readers will explore the latest trends shaping Kafka's development, along with future directions that promise to expand Kafka's capabilities.

Kafka in the Age of Cloud-Native Architectures

The adoption of cloud-native architectures has transformed how applications are developed, deployed, and managed. Kafka's integration with containerization, microservices, and cloud platforms allows organizations to deploy scalable, resilient data streaming solutions.

- **Kafka on Kubernetes and Containerized Environments**
- Overview of deploying Kafka on Kubernetes, leveraging container orchestration for scalability, resilience, and easier management.
- Best practices for running Kafka in Kubernetes, including resource allocation, network configurations, and scaling strategies.
- Tools and frameworks like Strimzi and Confluent Operator that simplify Kafka deployments on Kubernetes.
- **Managed Kafka Services in the Cloud**

- Overview of managed Kafka services offered by cloud providers, including AWS MSK, Azure Event Hubs, and Confluent Cloud.
- Advantages and trade-offs of managed Kafka services versus self-hosted deployments, including cost, control, and operational complexity.
- Example use cases for managed Kafka, such as short-term projects, applications with highly variable loads, and organizations with limited operational resources.
- **Serverless Architectures and Kafka**
- How Kafka fits into serverless architectures and the role of event-driven functions in a Kafka-based serverless system.
- Examples of using serverless frameworks, such as AWS Lambda, with Kafka to create event-driven workflows that scale automatically based on demand.
- Use cases for combining Kafka with serverless components, such as IoT data processing, lightweight analytics, and asynchronous processing tasks.

Event-Driven Architectures and the Future of Microservices

Kafka's pub-sub model has made it central to event-driven microservices. As event-driven architecture (EDA) becomes more popular, Kafka continues to evolve with new patterns and tools to support more complex workflows and real-time data processing.

- **Kafka's Role in Evolving Event-Driven Architectures**
- Overview of Kafka's role in EDA and how it supports asynchronous, decoupled interactions between microservices.
- Emerging trends in EDA, such as event streaming versus event sourcing and the move toward stateful versus stateless services.
- Examples of how Kafka enables modern EDA patterns, like choreographed workflows, CQRS, and transactional outboxes.
- **Improving Microservices Coordination with Kafka**
- Techniques for using Kafka to manage distributed transactions, long-running workflows, and inter-service communication.

- Patterns like the saga pattern, where Kafka coordinates workflows across multiple services without a centralized orchestrator.
- Example of an e-commerce application using Kafka to handle order processing, payment, and inventory management.
- **Real-Time Microservices with Kafka Streams and ksqlDB**
- Using Kafka Streams and ksqlDB to process data within microservices for real-time decision-making and analytics.
- Explanation of ksqlDB as an event streaming database built on Kafka, allowing SQL-based data processing in Kafka streams.
- Case study example of a real-time analytics system that uses Kafka Streams to process and respond to live data.

Real-Time Machine Learning with Kafka

Kafka is playing an increasingly important role in real-time machine learning (ML) and AI applications. By connecting data sources to ML pipelines and delivering real-time predictions, Kafka enables businesses to leverage machine learning insights as data flows.

- **Building Real-Time Machine Learning Pipelines with Kafka**
- Overview of Kafka's role in ML pipelines, including data ingestion, feature extraction, and real-time model serving.
- Example of a real-time ML pipeline where Kafka serves as the data backbone, feeding raw data into an ML model for live predictions.
- Explanation of the data preprocessing steps that can be handled directly within Kafka, reducing latency for real-time predictions.
- **Kafka for Online Learning and Model Updates**
- Techniques for implementing online learning (incremental model updates) in Kafka-based pipelines, enabling models to improve as new data arrives.
- Examples of how Kafka can manage the flow of new training data, triggering model retraining and updates in real time.
- Practical use cases of online learning with Kafka, such as personalization engines, fraud detection, and predictive maintenance.

- **Integrating Kafka with Popular ML and AI Frameworks**
- Overview of Kafka integrations with popular ML frameworks, including TensorFlow, PyTorch, and Spark MLlib.
- Techniques for deploying Kafka in conjunction with ML platforms to build scalable, low-latency ML workflows.
- Example of using Kafka with Apache Spark for distributed ML processing, allowing data preprocessing and model serving in a single pipeline.

Beyond Kafka: Alternatives and Complementary Tools

While Kafka is a powerful platform for data streaming, new tools and technologies have emerged that either complement or provide alternatives to Kafka in specific use cases. This section explores when Kafka is the best choice and when other tools might be better suited.

- **Comparing Kafka with Emerging Streaming Technologies**
- Overview of Apache Pulsar, RabbitMQ, and AWS Kinesis, and how they compare to Kafka in terms of scalability, latency, and ease of use.
- Strengths and limitations of each platform, including use cases where they may outperform Kafka.
- Example scenarios where alternatives to Kafka may be preferable, such as low-latency event processing with RabbitMQ or geo-replication with Pulsar.
- **Using Kafka with Complementary Tools**
- Explanation of complementary tools that extend Kafka's capabilities, such as Flink for advanced stream processing and Presto for real-time SQL analytics on Kafka data.
- Practical guide to integrating Kafka with a data lake or data warehouse, using tools like Apache Hudi or Delta Lake to enable scalable data storage and querying.
- Case study example of a Kafka-Flink pipeline for fraud detection, where Kafka handles event ingestion and Flink processes streaming data in real time.
- **The Future of Event Streaming: Combining Kafka with Edge**

Computing and IoT
- How Kafka is adapting to support edge computing and IoT applications, which require local processing for low latency and scalability.
- Explanation of Kafka's potential in edge environments, enabling local processing of IoT data and reducing network dependency.
- Examples of Kafka's role in IoT applications that require hybrid edge-to-cloud data processing, such as autonomous vehicles and smart manufacturing.

Future Directions and Innovations in Kafka

Kafka's roadmap includes ongoing improvements and features to address new challenges in data streaming, scalability, and observability. This section will explore Kafka's upcoming capabilities and potential areas of innovation.

- **Enhancements in Kafka's Scalability and Performance**
- Overview of Kafka's roadmap for scaling improvements, including increased partition count and faster replication protocols.
- Explanation of potential performance enhancements, such as tiered storage and improved indexing, to manage larger data volumes without impacting throughput.
- **Improving Kafka's Observability and Monitoring**
- New developments in Kafka's monitoring tools to offer better visibility into Kafka clusters, consumer lag, and data latency.
- Potential improvements in traceability and diagnostics to help users identify and resolve issues in distributed Kafka deployments.
- Emerging tools and standards, such as OpenTelemetry, that enhance Kafka's observability in multi-cloud and hybrid environments.
- **Event Streaming in the Context of Data Privacy and Compliance**
- How Kafka is evolving to support data privacy regulations like GDPR and CCPA, including new features for data governance and audit trails.
- Future capabilities for managing data retention, encryption, and access controls to comply with increasingly stringent data privacy requirements.
- Best practices for implementing data anonymization and ensuring

compliance while maintaining Kafka's streaming capabilities.

Practical Exercises and Case Studies

To illustrate the emerging trends and future directions discussed in this chapter, this section includes practical exercises and case studies that allow readers to explore Kafka's latest capabilities.

- **Exercise: Deploying Kafka on Kubernetes for a Scalable Microservices Architecture**
- Step-by-step guide to setting up Kafka on Kubernetes, using tools like Strimzi to manage Kafka deployments in a containerized environment.
- Instructions for scaling Kafka to support a microservices architecture, demonstrating how Kafka facilitates event-driven interactions between services.
- **Case Study: Real-Time Machine Learning Pipeline with Kafka and TensorFlow**
- Detailed case study of building a real-time ML pipeline using Kafka and TensorFlow, covering data ingestion, feature extraction, model serving, and real-time predictions.
- Example of how the pipeline can be configured to deliver instant recommendations or alerts based on real-time data.
- **Exercise: Setting Up a Kafka-Flink Pipeline for Edge Computing**
- Practical exercise on setting up Kafka and Apache Flink for an edge computing use case, such as real-time data analysis for IoT devices.
- Step-by-step guide to processing data locally with Flink and sending only processed insights to a centralized Kafka cluster for analysis and storage.

Building Real-Time Data Analytics with Kafka

Incorporating real-time data analytics into business processes provides actionable insights and enables organizations to respond instantly to changing conditions. Kafka's ability to handle high-throughput data streams makes it an ideal foundation for real-time analytics. This chapter covers how to design and implement a Kafka-based analytics pipeline, from data ingestion and transformation to visualization, using Kafka in conjunction with analytics and monitoring tools.

Setting Up a Real-Time Analytics Platform with Kafka

Building a real-time analytics platform involves setting up Kafka as the primary data ingestion and processing layer, allowing data to be transformed and analyzed as it flows through the pipeline.

- **Key Components of a Real-Time Analytics Platform**
- Overview of the core components needed for real-time analytics: data ingestion, stream processing, storage, and visualization.
- Explanation of Kafka's role in the pipeline, serving as the main conduit for streaming data between sources, processing engines, and analytics tools.
- **Designing a Scalable Kafka Architecture for Analytics**
- Best practices for setting up Kafka in a real-time analytics context, including partitioning strategies, replication, and topic organization.

- Tips for configuring Kafka to handle high-throughput data streams, ensuring low latency and minimal data loss.
- Example architecture for an analytics pipeline that ingests data from multiple sources, processes it in real time, and outputs insights to dashboards and data lakes.
- **Configuring Kafka Connect for Data Ingestion**
- Using Kafka Connect to import data from external sources, such as databases, log files, and APIs.
- Example connectors for popular data sources in analytics, such as JDBC for databases and HTTP for APIs.
- Practical example of setting up Kafka Connect to continuously ingest data into Kafka for real-time processing and analysis.

Real-Time Data Processing and Transformation with Kafka Streams

Kafka Streams provides an in-platform method for real-time data processing, enabling transformations, aggregations, and filtering without the need for external tools.

- **Transforming Data with Kafka Streams**
- Using Kafka Streams to transform raw data, such as converting JSON logs into structured data or normalizing metrics for analysis.
- Practical examples of common transformations in analytics, including data enrichment, reformatting, and filtering irrelevant data.
- **Real-Time Aggregations for Analytics**
- Explanation of how to perform real-time aggregations in Kafka Streams, such as calculating moving averages, counts, and totals.
- Setting up windows in Kafka Streams to analyze data over specific time frames, allowing for metrics like hourly counts or daily summaries.
- Example of aggregating user activity data to provide real-time insights into application performance and usage.
- **Integrating Machine Learning Models with Kafka Streams**
- Explanation of how to use Kafka Streams to apply machine learning models in real-time, such as for predictive analytics or anomaly detection.

- Techniques for scoring data in real time by connecting Kafka Streams to model-serving frameworks or using pre-trained models directly in stream processors.
- Example of a real-time sentiment analysis application where Kafka Streams processes social media data and classifies it based on sentiment scores.

Visualizing Real-Time Data with Grafana, Kibana, and Tableau

Visualizing real-time data is crucial for making insights actionable. Kafka integrates well with various visualization and monitoring tools, allowing users to build dashboards and generate real-time reports.

- **Setting Up Grafana for Kafka Monitoring and Visualization**
- Step-by-step guide to connecting Grafana to Kafka metrics and creating dashboards for real-time insights.
- Example of visualizing key Kafka metrics, such as consumer lag, message throughput, and partition utilization, to monitor system health.
- Building business-specific dashboards, such as user engagement tracking or product performance metrics, with Kafka as the data source.
- **Using Kibana for Real-Time Log and Event Analysis**
- Integrating Kafka with the Elastic Stack (ELK), specifically with Kibana, to visualize and analyze event data and logs in real time.
- Practical example of setting up a real-time log analysis pipeline, where Kafka ingests application logs and Kibana provides a searchable, visual interface.
- Tips for configuring Kibana alerts based on Kafka metrics, enabling proactive monitoring and incident response.
- **Tableau for Real-Time Business Analytics**
- Overview of using Tableau to create real-time business dashboards, with Kafka as the data ingestion layer.
- Techniques for connecting Tableau to Kafka topics or using Kafka Connect to push data into Tableau-compatible formats (such as databases or data warehouses).

- Example of a real-time sales dashboard in Tableau, pulling data from Kafka to track sales metrics and customer behavior.

Case Study: Implementing a Real-Time Dashboard
A case study provides a complete example of a real-time analytics system powered by Kafka, from data ingestion and processing to visualization and alerting.

- **End-to-End Pipeline Design**
- Detailed architecture of the case study pipeline, including Kafka for data ingestion, Kafka Streams for transformation, and Grafana/Kibana for visualization.
- Explanation of the data flow, from raw event ingestion to transformed metrics displayed on a live dashboard.
- **Real-World Application Example**
- Example use case: a website performance monitoring system that tracks real-time user interactions, identifies traffic spikes, and alerts administrators.
- Explanation of how Kafka handles different data types, including log events, clickstream data, and server metrics.
- **Testing and Scaling the Analytics Pipeline**
- Techniques for load testing the Kafka-based analytics pipeline to ensure it can handle production data volumes.
- Scaling strategies for each component, including partitioning for Kafka topics and horizontal scaling of Kafka Streams applications.

Practical Exercises and Hands-On Examples
To solidify readers' understanding, this section provides hands-on exercises focused on building a real-time analytics pipeline with Kafka, performing transformations with Kafka Streams, and creating visualizations.

- **Exercise: Building a Simple Real-Time Analytics Pipeline**
- Step-by-step guide to setting up a basic analytics pipeline with Kafka,

from data ingestion to transformation and visualization.

- Instructions for connecting Kafka to Grafana or Kibana, creating a dashboard for visualizing processed data.
- **Exercise: Implementing Real-Time Aggregations with Kafka Streams**
- Exercise on setting up a Kafka Streams application to aggregate data in real time, such as counting website clicks or calculating moving averages.
- Sample code and configurations to demonstrate windowed aggregations and data processing within Kafka.
- **Exercise: Setting Up a Real-Time Alert System with Kafka and Grafana**
- Practical exercise on configuring Kafka and Grafana to monitor real-time metrics and send alerts for threshold breaches.
- Example of creating alerts for specific conditions, such as high consumer lag or message throughput, allowing users to proactively manage the Kafka pipeline.